MA…
in the
U.S.A.

A Guide

By Marsha Bellavance-Johnson

Illustrated by T.H. Johnson

Published by
THE COMPUTER LAB
Box 4300
Ketchum, Idaho 83340

FAMOUS FOOTSTEPS™

guide booklets
about famous people
in their favorite places

Titles available:

Kit Carson in the West

Emily Dickinson in Amherst

Ernest Hemingway in Idaho

Ernest Hemingway in Key West

Georgia O'Keeffe in New Mexico

Mark Twain in the U.S.A.

Tennessee Williams in Key West and Miami

Front cover photo: Mark Twain in his library at Stormfield, in 1908, Redding, Connecticut. Courtesy Beinecke Rare Book Library, Yale University.

Back cover photo: Mark Twain at 35, when this photo was taken in 1871. Courtesy Library of Congress.

ISBN 0-929-70907-1

First Edition

printed by
Sun Litho
USA

TABLE OF CONTENTS

NOTE TO READERS

I hope readers will find this brief guide to Mark Twain in the U.S.A. helpful. Mark Twain was one of America's greatest citizens. During his lifetime he was a printer, steamboat pilot, soldier, miner, reporter, traveler, lecturer, inventor, publisher, editor, businessman, husband, father and humorist. His greatest fame is as the author of such immortal works as *The Adventures of Tom Sawyer*, *The Adventures of Huckleberry Finn*, *The Innocents Abroad*, and *The Prince and the Pauper*. His birth in 1835 coincided with Halley's comet, as did his death in 1910.

Mark Twain traveled all over the world, truly remarkable in his time and impressive even today. His wanderlust continued into his old age. His social commentary frequently seems as appropriate today as when it was written. His stories about the Army Corps of Engineers in *Life on the Mississippi*, or hyped-up investors and politicans in *The Gilded Age* make one realize how little some things have changed.

It is this timeless quality which stimulates Mark Twain celebrations, events and commemorations from California to Connecticut. There are schools, museums, hotels, streets, shopping centers even a hospital, saloon and library named after him. For serious scholars the Mark Twain Project is headquartered in the Bancroft Library at the University of California at Berkeley.

People planning to travel to any of the areas written about should try to read the Twain related works before or during their travels. A drive from Missouri to San Francisco would be greatly enhanced by a reading of *Roughing It* and *The Innocents Abroad* is a must for the Mediterranean bound.

Many people have helped with this booklet. Those deserving special mention include: John Cunning, Henry Sweets, James Hefley, James Caron, Sandy Umemoto, Darryl Baskin, Constance Barone, Gayle Early, Peter Salwen, John Vincent Boyer, Helen Stauderman, Kay Reinehr, William Loos, Rick Berby, Susan Snyder, Lee Bellavance, and Kenneth Hulme. I especially want to thank Mrs. John (Doris) Meaney, Mrs. Norman (Pat) Malboeuf and Mrs. Francois (Martha) Bellavance.

INTRODUCTION

Samuel Langhorne Clemens was born in the small frontier village of Florida, Missouri on November 30, 1835. By the time he died 74 years later he was known and loved the world over as Mark Twain, author, riverboat pilot, miner, reporter, traveler, publisher, inventor and lecturer. His life was a fascinating adventure with many occupations in many places. He enjoyed fame and wealth but also the pain of great business and personal losses.

The Clemens family had frequently traveled the distance between great expectations and disillusionment, between high hopes and despair. The family owned 70,000 acres of land in Tennessee but it brought nothing except the hope of prospective wealth that never materialized. The father, John Marshall Clemens was a lawyer and storekeeper who married Jane Lampton and brought her to Missouri. He had high hopes that a canal would link the Salt River in Florida, Missouri with the commerce on the Mississippi. He bought land, set up a shop and became a judge in that tiny hamlet. The family occupied a modest home/cabin (see page 13) where their sixth child Samuel arrived with Halley's comet on November 30, 1835. In 1839, when Florida had not prospered as anticipated, John Clemens bought property and moved the family forty miles to the town of Hannibal, Missouri (see page 15) on the Mississippi River.

The river, local characters, their adventures and the places in and around Hannibal have been immortalized in such books as *The Adventures of Tom Sawyer*, *The Adventures of Huckleberry Finn*, and *Life on the Mississippi*. The farm of his uncle John Quarles, near Florida, Missouri, where Sam spent his childhood summers was also a source for his stories.

In Hannibal, young Sam Clemens attended three different schools including Sunday school. He generally disliked schooling, although he could spell well. He really did know Laura Hawkins who was the model for Becky Thatcher and whose house still stands in Hannibal.

Compared to the tiny village of Florida, the small town of Hannibal was a bustling metropolis. There were meat packing plants, barrel makers, taverns, churches and shops. Surrounded by woods and right on the Mississippi River, the town was a "boy's paradise".

Judge Clemens practiced law (his office in Hannibal has been restored) but the family finances were never adequate. In 1844 he built a modest house on Hill Street which was the scene of Tom Sawyer's boyhood adventures. But Judge Clemens was unable to support even that house and the family was forced to board with the Grant family in the House of the Pilasters. It was in that house that the childhood of Sam Clemens came to an abrupt end in 1847 when his father died leaving his mother an impoverished widow. Sam had to support himself and was sent to apprentice as a printer with Joseph Ament of Hannibal when only thirteen.

In 1849 or 1850 Sam's brother Orion purchased a paper in Hannibal, the *Journal* and Sam went to work there. Unfortunately Orion seemed to have inherited the business sense of his father and almost all his enterprises were financial failures. Sam occasionally wrote for his brother's paper and is also the supposed author of a comic piece which appeared in a Boston weekly in 1852.

In 1853, with his brother's paper failing, Samuel Clemens left Hannibal. He headed east and did typesetting in New York City (see page 33). He was especially attracted by America's first World's Fair. Then he went on to another itinerant printing job in Philidelphia and even visited Washington, D.C. in 1854 (see page 35). His travel letters, published by Orion in the Muscatine, Iowa *Journal*, demonstrate an uncanny ability to perceive and describe the essential qualities of his surroundings.

In 1854 he was back in Missouri working as a typesetter in St. Louis. The following year he joined his younger brother Henry in Keokuk, Iowa at Orion's Ben Franklin Book and Job Printing Office. Even today an early portrait of Mark Twain hangs in the Keokuk Public Library which is only about 60 miles from Hannibal. The library is also a Mark Twain Center and usually has a summer exhibit of Twain memorabilia. After a year and a half in Keokuk (having been virtually unpaid) he decided to seek his fortunes in the Brazilian Amazon. In later years he returned to Keokuk, both to lecture and visit family.

In April, 1857 Samuel Clemens boarded the steamship *Paul Jones* headed for New Orleans, his first step toward South America. But he never got there. Before reaching New Orleans, he had totally altered his course. As a child he had dreamed of being a pilot on the mighty Mississippi (see page 17). That desire was rekindled and he convinced the ship's pilot, Horace Bixby to teach him the river for five hundred dollars. His remembrances of those days, as an apprentice and pilot, were published twenty-five years later in *Life on the*

Mississippi. Samuel Clemens loved being a well-paid pilot on the grand Mississippi steamboats. But the Civil War put a halt to most of the river traffic. By 1861 he was off the river. It would take eight years of hard work before he would again achieve the status, prestige and income of his riverboat days.

He then joined a group of "irregular" Confederate soldiers who called themselves the Marion Rangers and who were planning to join a regular force. After two weeks he deserted that group in favor of "government service" in the west.

After Lincoln's election, Sam's brother, Orion had been appointed Secretary to the Nevada Territory. Sam became the unofficial secretary to the Secretary and both brothers were on a stagecoach heading west by July of 1861. His fascinating account of that trip west was later published as *Roughing It.*

Carson City (see page 19), capital of the Nevada Territory was the initial destination. Once there Sam was intrigued by the promises of wealth that the west seemed to offer. He tried being a timber-man, miner, speculator and newsman in the hopes of striking it rich but was barely able to support himself.

Lake Tahoe, only about 12 miles away was the scene of his first venture. He had heard of the "marvellous beauty" of the lake which he described in chapters 22 and 23 of his book *Roughing It.* His plan was to make a fortune supplying timber for the mines and he staked some claims. He camped on the north shore for several weeks while he and his partners built a primitive shelter. He felt the water was too cold for swimming but was astounded by its clarity. Unfortunately, he started a forest fire and the plan for a wood ranch went up in smoke.

Next the lure of gold and silver sent him prospecting in the Humbolt and Esmeralda districts. He spent time at Mono Lake and in Aurora. The mining itself was hard work especially since he considered himself lazy. He tried stock speculation but that required insider knowledge, money and luck which he never seemed to have simultaneously.

Too much hard work combined with too little luck sent him scurrying to make a living. With his next step he would start a new life - with a new name! He walked 130 miles to accept an offer as a staff reporter for the *Daily Territorial Enterprise* in the booming mining town of Virginia City, Nevada (see page 21). He even covered the Territorial Legislature in Carson City. Soon he was signing his articles with the by-line Mark Twain (a common practice of the times was to use pen names). There are several versions of how he acquired the name. Mark twain means two fathoms and was an expression of the leadsman on ship which meant the water was deep enough for the ship. Another version is that it was the expression he would use when telling the barkeeps of Virginia City to add two drinks to his account. In his *Autobiography* he claimed to have stolen the name from an old Mississippi pilot, Captain Sellers, but there is no evidence that Captain Sellers ever used that name.

Whatever its source, from then on his writings were published using the alias Mark Twain. By then he had also grown his bushy mustache and was a heavy smoker and drinker and a prankster too. But soon there was trouble in Virginia City. Trying to write a joke article, Twain had offended many of the female uppercrust by suggesting that a fund raising effort was to support miscegenation. To avoid trouble and even the possibility of a duel Twain left for San Francisco (see page 25) on May 29, 1864.

When he first arrived in San Francisco he enjoyed the pleasures of the city and lived like a wealthy man. But his mining shares did not appreciate as anticipated. Twain was forced to work as a local reporter for the *Daily Morning Call* from June until October of 1864. During that time he wrote several hundred articles about the city on a wide range of topics from prostitutes to politics He was under a lot of work pressure and was not allowed to be as creative with the facts as he had been in Virginia City. Eventually he was relieved of his position. At times he was nearly penniless. But he had literary connections and friends such as Bret Harte, and was soon writing for other publications. One day he went to aid a friend involved in a brawl. He realized afterwards that it might be best to leave the city until things cooled down, especially since the authorities were not happy about some articles he had written exposing police corruption

In December of 1864 he left San Francico for the Gillis cabin on Jackass Hill (see page 27) in the Mother Lode Country. He was a miner once again. The hard work, mud, deprivation and lack of success nearly drove him to suicide. Early in 1865 he was in nearby Angels Camp (see page 29) and heard a story about a jumping frog. Using the old tale as a basis, he created his famous story "The Celebrated Jumping Frog of Calaveras County" which was published in the east in November of 1865 and won him his first national fame.

By March of 1866 he left mining forever and embarked on a trip to the Sandwich Islands (see Hawaii, page 31). He was on assignment to send travel letters to the Sacramento *Daily Union*. The letters were popular and his one month trip was extended to four months! For many years he used that material for his lectures. Today the *Union* remains proud of its Twain connection: there is a bust of him in the lobby exhibit at the *Union* building in Old Sacramento. Twain's success as a travel writer secured him his next assignment: reporting about a luxury Mediterranean cruise aboard the *Quaker City*.

Before leaving on the cruise he was in New York City (see page 33) where he gave his Hawaii lecture at Cooper Union in May of 1867. A few days later he left for Europe. His letters to the *Alta California* about the trip to Europe and the Holy Land were a great success. When he returned in the fall of 1867 he got a position with Senator Stewart of Nevada in Washington, D.C.. In March of 1868 he had to make a quick trip west, his last time in California, to arrange for the rights to use his *Quaker City* letters. Back in Washington, he worked on developing the letters into a book, *The Innocents Abroad*. Published in 1869, the book catapulted its author into fame and established his career.

There were significant developments in Twain's personal life also. He had fallen in love with Olivia "Livy" Langdon of Elmira, New York (see pages 37 and 43). His was a hectic pace, with writing, lecturing, and courting Livy. They were married in 1870. His new father-in-law surprised him with an elegant home on Delaware Avenue in Buffalo as a wedding gift. Twain had purchased into the Buffalo *Express* and the young couple commenced a happy married life together. Twain wrote for his paper and started work on several books. But his father-in-law soon fell ill and died in August. Also in 1870 his first child, a son, Langdon was born. Langdon was always sickly and died in 1872. Twain had been a member of the Buffalo and Erie County Public Library from 1869 to 1872. In 1885 the library requested a manuscript from him. The first half of that *Huckleberry Finn* manuscript, missing for over a hundred years has recently been found. The library has a special *Huckleberry Finn* collection which scholars may arrange to research.

In 1871 the family moved to Hartford (see page 39). The next two decades were to be the most happy and productive years of his life. He went on a lecture tour in 1872. He did a lot of writing, especially during summers at Quarry Farm in Elmira, New York (see page 37). In the decade that followed he wrote *Roughing It, The Gilded Age, The Adventures of Tom Sawyer, A Tramp Abroad* and *The Prince and the Pauper.* He often worked on several books at a time and would sometimes put something aside for years. He also obtained some patents on inventions like the self-adhesive scrapbook.

In 1878 he even toured in Germany and lived in Europe with his family for sixteen months.

Life in Hartford resumed with gusto and William Dean Howells reported having to recover from the late nights, smoking and drinking after visiting in Hartford.

An especially significant year was 1884. In that year his company published President Grant's *Personal Memories, The Adventures of Huckleberry Finn* was published, and he did a lecture tour. He also was interested in the Paige typesetting machine, which would become a disaster for him.

In 1888 he received the first of his honorary degrees, a Master of Arts from Yale University. He was still living in Hartford and working on *A Connecticut Yankee in King Arthur's Court.*

The Paige typesetter had become a real financial drain and the family was hard pressed. In 1891 they moved to Europe where they could live more economically. They spent a year in Florence then two years in France, although Twain claimed not to have learned to speak French. He did however make many business trips back to the States. The stock market crash of 1893 was a severe blow. He was rescused by Henry Rogers of Standard Oil, who became a friend and patron.

A world lecture tour in 1895 and 1896 was immensely popular and earned much needed money. The family was planning a reunion when word was received that his daughter, Susy Clemens, had died unexpectedly in Hartford. The following years were to be filled with unhappiness. From then on, his writing seemed more cynical and pessimistic

Twain did not return to the United States for five years. During that time he published *Personal Recollections of Joan of Arc* in 1896 and *Following the Equator* in 1897. While in Europe he had been treated like a celebrity and received by royalty. He was equally well treated when he returned to America to live in New York City in 1900. His ship was met by many old friends and news reporters. For the next ten years it seems that hundreds of newspaper articles were written about Mark Twain.

In 1902 Mark Twain made his last visit to Missouri, to accept an honorary degree from the University of Missouri. He went on to visit in Hannibal where he gave an unexpected commencement address to the Hannibal High School class of 1902. He visited with Laura Hawkins and they had dinner at the Garth house.

His wife Livy had long suffered from a heart condition and was in poor health. Thinking that the Italian sunshine would revive her, they left their home in Riverdale, New York and went to Florence in 1903. Olivia Langdon Clemens died there on June 5, 1904. Twain was heartbroken.

He then moved to 21 Fifth Avenue in New York City where he had his huge Venetian bed brought in 1904. From that bed he would often receive visitors, give interviews, write letters for his biography and read. One of the social events of the season in New York was the Mark Twain birthday gala at Delmonico's in 1905.

He had thought he would never return to Europe, but an honorary degree from Oxford changed his mind and he went to England to accept the degree personally in 1907. In 1906 he had purchased 200 acres in Redding, Connecticut (see page 41) and was having a large home built there. He moved to Redding in 1908. His first year there was a happy one. His daughter Clara was married and he wore his Oxford robes for the occasion. But tragedy struck again. Daughter Jean died on Christmas Eve, 1909. This was the final blow for Twain. He spent the next few months in Bermuda but was increasingly ill and returned home on April 14.

He had been born with Halley's Comet and now he wanted to go out with it. On April 21, 1910 Samuel L. Clemens, known the world over as Mark Twain, died at his home "Stormfield" in Redding, Connecticut. Overhead Halley's comet lit the night sky.

Crowds thronged his funeral which was held at the Brick Presbyterian Church on Fifth Avenue. He is buried with his family in Elmira, New York.

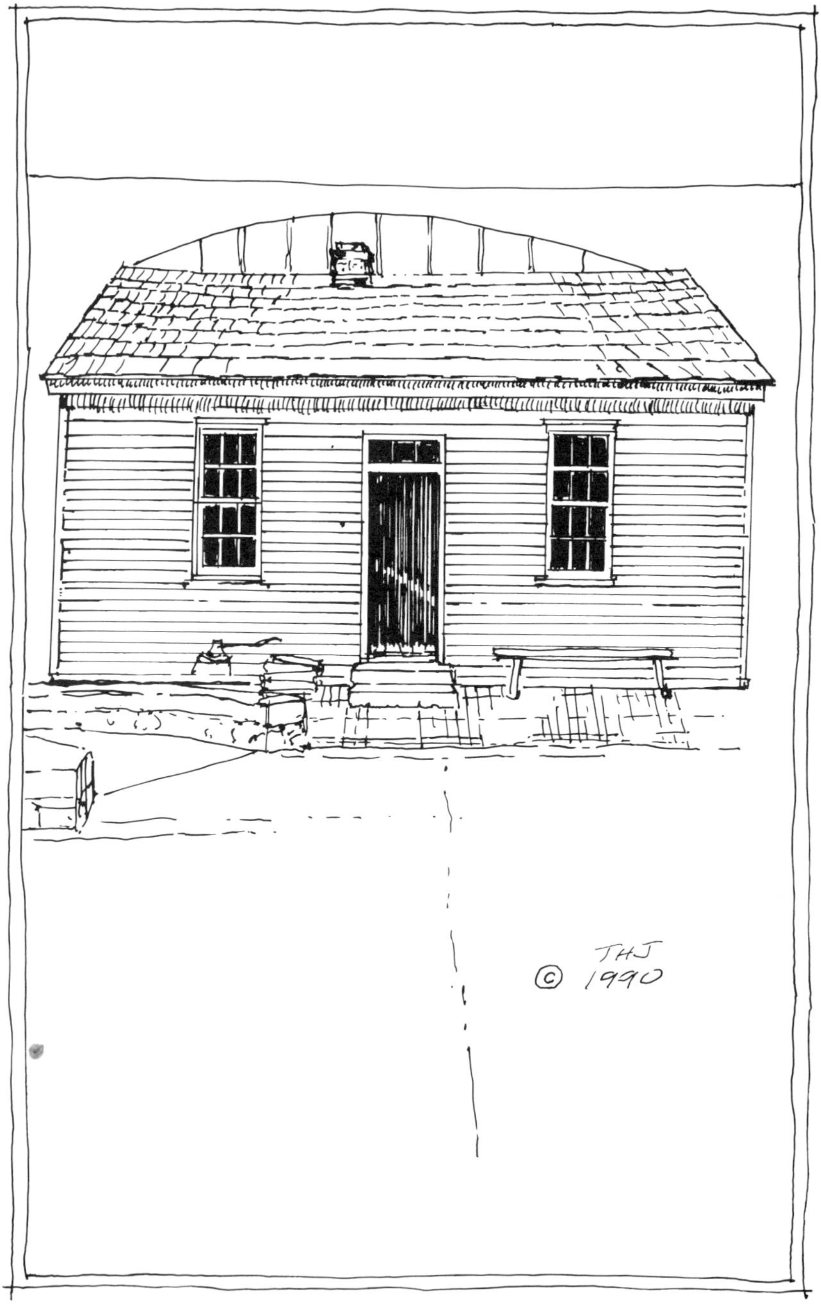
THJ
© 1990

FLORIDA

Florida, Missouri was and probably always will be a tiny community, removed from the bustle of tourism and commerce. It is located about 40 miles southwest of Hannibal via routes 36 west and 24 west to 107 south. Here, on November 30, 1835 Samuel Langhorne Clemens was born two months prematurely, in a modest two room cabin. Above, Halley's comet streaked across the sky.

The Clemens family had recently moved from Tennessee in the hopes of finding prosperity. John Clemens speculated in local land, opened a shop, practiced law, became a local judge and supported development of the Salt River.

When little business materialized Judge Clemens moved his family to Hannibal, Missouri in 1839 (see page 15). But that was not the end of Samuel Clemens in Florida. His Uncle John Quarles owned a nearby farm where young Sam spent most of his childhood summers. Events and people at the farm were portrayed in later works. The character and dialect of Jim in *Huckleberry Finn* is based on Uncle Dan'l, a slave on the Quarles family farm.

Today the birthplace cabin is located INSIDE a modern museum at the Mark Twain State Park and Historic Site off of Route 107 near Stoutsville. The museum was built in 1960 and contains Twain artifacts, including some first editions, films, and a handwritten manuscript of *Tom Sawyer*. A small library and public reading room are available for research. There is an excellent 18-minute slide show and a full-size replica of a steamboat pilothouse. Admission is $1.25 for adults, $.75 for children up to twelve and free for those under six. The museum is open almost every day. For more information call (314) 565-3449.

Outside picnic tables overlook the Mark Twain Lake, although no food is for sale in the immediate museum area. About one quarter mile north of the historic site, near the boundary of the Mark Twain State Park a plaque marks the original site of the birthplace cabin. Nearby Florida Cemetery contains the grave of Sam's sister, Margaret Clemens.

In 1983 the Clarence Cannon Dam on the Salt River created the Mark Twain Lake which abounds with recreational opportunities such as fishing, swimming, boating and camping. There is even a beach in the Mark Twain State Park. For information call the Mark Twain Lake Association at (314) 565-2228.

THJ
© 1991

HANNIBAL

Hannibal, Missouri is on the Mississippi River about one hundred miles north of St. Louis. This was the scene of Sam Clemens' boyhood adventures and the setting for Mark Twain's books *The Adventures of Tom Sawyer* and *Huckleberry Finn.*

The Clemens family had moved to Hannibal in 1839. They did not prosper but, surrounded by thick woods and a constant stream of river traffic, the environment was "a boy's paradise".

Today Hannibal is filled with evidence of its Samuel Clemens/Mark Twain heritage. The Mark Twain boyhood home, where the family lived until 1853, was completely restored in 1990 (sketch on opposite page). A replica of the fence painted by Tom Sawyer and his friends is there too. The adjoining Mark Twain Museum and Visitor Center offers exhibits and a slide show. Across the street the Clemens Law Office and the "Becky Thatcher" house, home of Sam's childhood sweetheart, have also been preserved. Her house now includes an excellent bookstore.

In 1846 financial problems forced the Clemens family to board with the Grant's in the now restored House of the Pilasters, where Judge Clemens died in 1847. After his father died, Sam was apprenticed to a printer and later worked for his brother on the *Journal*, a local paper. Samuel Clemens left Hannibal in 1853 but returned for visits until 1902.

A twenty-minute tour on the horse-drawn Mark Twain Clopper or an hour tour on the open-air Twainland Express "train" provide comfortable sightseeing. Tourists can also climb Cardiff Hill at the base of which is a statue of Tom and Huck. Other sights include the Tom Sawyer Dioramas Museum, the Haunted House on Hill Street, the Garth Woodside Mansion, the Rockcliffe Mansion, the Mark Twain Riverboat trip, the Molly Brown Dinner Theatre and the Mark Twain Outdoor Theatre. There is also a statue of Mark Twain in Riverview Park. The Mark Twain Cave offers tours in the same caves where Tom Sawyer and Becky Thatcher were lost! The National Tom Sawyer Days, a 4th of July event, includes a fence painting contest and a frog jump. Many businesses, a bridge, a road and even a school are named after him! The Hannibal-LaGrange Community College sponsors an annual Mark Twain Writers Conference.

For additional information, contact the Hannibal Visitors Bureau at (314) 221-2477.

MARK TWAIN RIVERBOAT CO.

HANNIBAL, MISSOURI

THE MISSISSIPPI

If there is any one thing with which Mark Twain is especially identified it's the image of steamboating on the Mississippi River. Samuel Clemens was only four years old when he moved with his family to the riverside town of Hannibal, Missouri (see page 15).

The river is prominent in Twain works such as *The Adventures of Tom Sawyer* and *The Adventures of Huckleberry Finn* which are set in Hannibal. The river was the main mode of transport for people, livestock, supplies and commerce. There were even huge showboats designed for entertainment. Having a procession of river traffic constantly floating by provided the youngsters of Hannibal entertainment and education. The swift currents and floods taught them about danger and death too.

The local boys fished, swam and boated on the river. Deserted Jackson Island offered an excellent hideaway. Excursion boats took parties for picnics and to explore the local caves. Samuel Clemens, like the other boys in town, dreamed of one day working on the river. For him that dream was to become a reality.

On a trip to New Orleans in 1857 He convinced Horace Bixby, the pilot of the *Paul Jones* to take him on as an apprentice. He learned the river from St. Louis to New Orleans and got his pilot's certificate in April of 1859. He loved his work as a pilot since the money, high status, travel and diversity suited his temperment. Unfortunately the Civil War halted most river traffic in 1861. Samuel Clemens was forced to leave the job he loved. It would be many years before he would again secure such a favorable position.

In 1882, Mark Twain traveled the river again seeking to refresh his memory for a book. Many of his early piloting adventures and comments about the river, people, politics and life are contained in *Life on the Mississippi.* This is must reading for anyone interested in, or planning a trip on the Mississippi.

Today riverboats are a popular tourist attraction, providing short trips, overnight trips, and dinner cruises. From Hannibal the riverboat *Mark Twain* takes thousands of tourists on short trips (call 800-621-2322). The famous *Delta Queen* offers cruises from New Orleans which stop in Hannibal (800-543-1949). It seems that millions in the world share that same vision of steamboats, the Mississippi and Mark Twain.

THJ
© 1991

CARSON CITY

Today Carson City is the capitol of the state of Nevada. When Samuel Clemens arrived via stagecoach in August of 1861 Carson City was a dusty frontier town and capitol city of the Nevada Territory. His brother, Orion Clemens, had been named Secretary to the Nevada Territory (often called Washoe). His own career as a Mississippi riverboat pilot had been interrupted by the Civil War, so he accompanied his brother as an unofficial secretary to the Secretary. They traveled westward over the Pony Express Route, experiences he later recalled in the book *Roughing It.*

While Orion Clemens was frequently called upon to be "Acting Governor" there was little to occupy Samuel Clemens. To earn his living he went to nearby Lake Tahoe were he staked some timber claims, planning to sell lumber to the mines. Those plans went up in smoke when he accidently started a forest fire.

Next, Samuel Clemens was struck with silver fever. The Nevada silver rush had started in 1859. He had high expectations and some financial backing from Orion. He speculated in mining shares as well as doing the dirty, strenuous mining itself. While prospecting in Aurora, in the Esmeralda district, he wrote some letters to the *Daily Territorial Enterprise* in Virginia City, Nevada which resulted in an offer of employment from that paper.

In 1862 he started work in Virginia City (see page 21) and soon began calling himself Mark Twain. He was frequently in Carson City, about 15 miles away, to report about the Territorial Legislature and to visit his brother. In 1863, Samuel Clemens was voted President of the Third House, a body devoted to parody of the legislature.

Samuel Clemens/Mark Twain was also a visitor at the old Ormsby House and casino which was several blocks away from the current Ormsby House. A model of the old hotel, a bar named after Mark Twain and a photo of him in the casino area recall his association with this establishment.

When in Carson City Samuel Clemens often stayed at the Orion Clemens house which is located at 502 N. Division Street, at the corner of Spear. There is a Nevada Historical Society marker at the house which was originally wood sided. It was stuccoed in the 1940's. Today the building is private property and NOT OPEN to the public; it contains law offices.

TERRITORIAL
THJ
© 1991

VIRGINIA CITY

Virginia City, Nevada is located on State Highway 341, about 15 miles from Carson City. It was here in 1862 that Samuel Clemens took a newspaper job with the *Daily Territorial Enterprise*. When he left nearly two years later he was the somewhat celebrated local writer known as Mark Twain, a navigation term meaning two fathoms (see introduction pages 7 and 8).

When Twain worked here Virginia City was a boom town stimulated by gold and silver mines. It was prosperous and sophisticated, full of saloons, restaurants, brothels, casinos, even an opera house. He met other writers like Dan de Quille and Artemus Ward. Newspapers were not as factual then and Twain was allowed great freedom with the "facts". He especially liked hoax stories in which he provided clues to the falsity of the story. Just such a joke article, in which he accused the ladies of Carson City of raising money for miscegenation, resulted in his hasty departure for San Francisco (see page 25) in May of 1864.

In October of 1866, after experiences in San Francisco, the California Gold Country (see pages 27 & 29) and The Sandwich Islands (see page 31) he was back in Virginia City where he gave a successful lecture at Piper's Opera House. After the speech his friends played a practical joke on him: they staged a fake hold-up on the "Divide" between Gold Hill and Virginia City. And finally in April of 1868, on his last trip west, he lectured about the Holy Land in Virginia City.

Today Virginia City has retained its honky-tonk boom town atmosphere. Instead of miners, it caters to tourists. The *Enterprise* as a newspaper is out of business but the building where he worked is still standing on "C" Street, marked by a plaque. It is a gift shop which is open daily and also contains a Mark Twain museum downstairs. Also on "C" Street: The Mark Twain Saloon and another Mark Twain Museum. The Chronicle Bookstore provides an assortment of books by and about Twain. During the summer Piper's Opera House (at the same site as the building where Twain lectured) features performances by a Mark Twain impersonator. From May through September San Francisco style tram cars provide 18-minute narrated tours of the historical city. For more information contact the Virginia City Chamber of Commerce at (702) 847-0311.

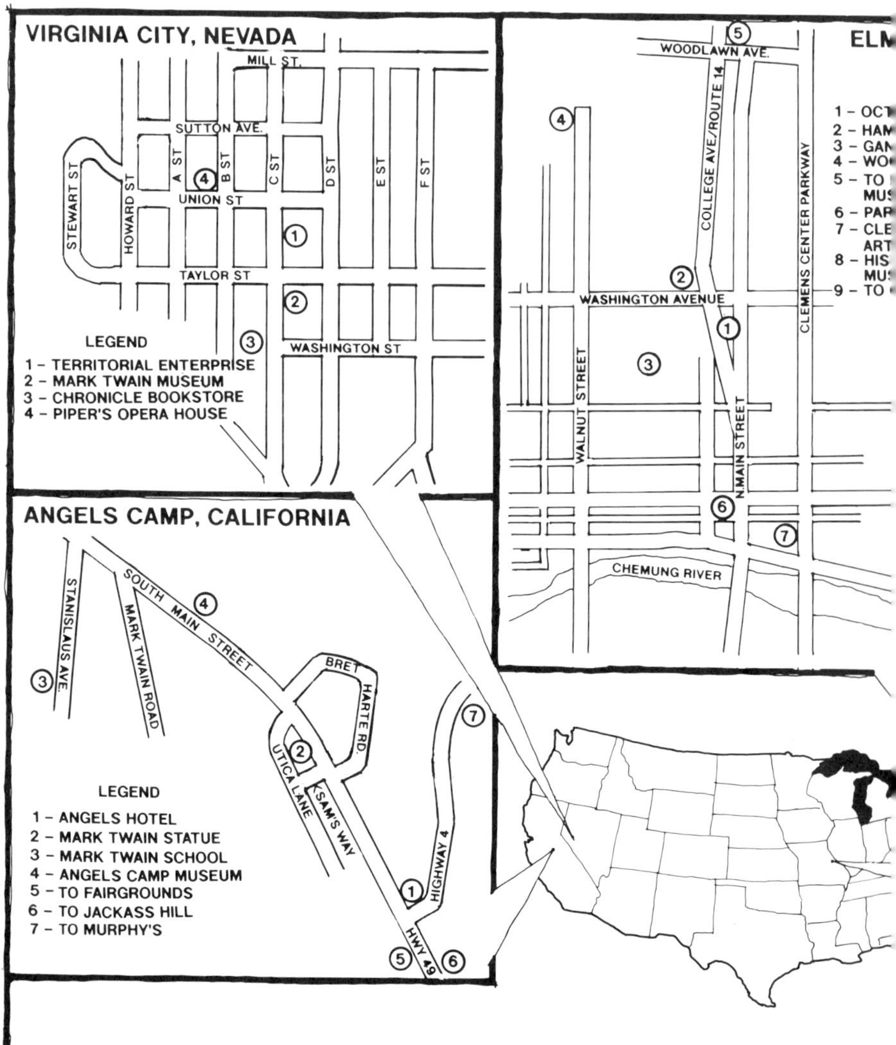

MAPS

MARK TWAIN IN THE U.S.A.

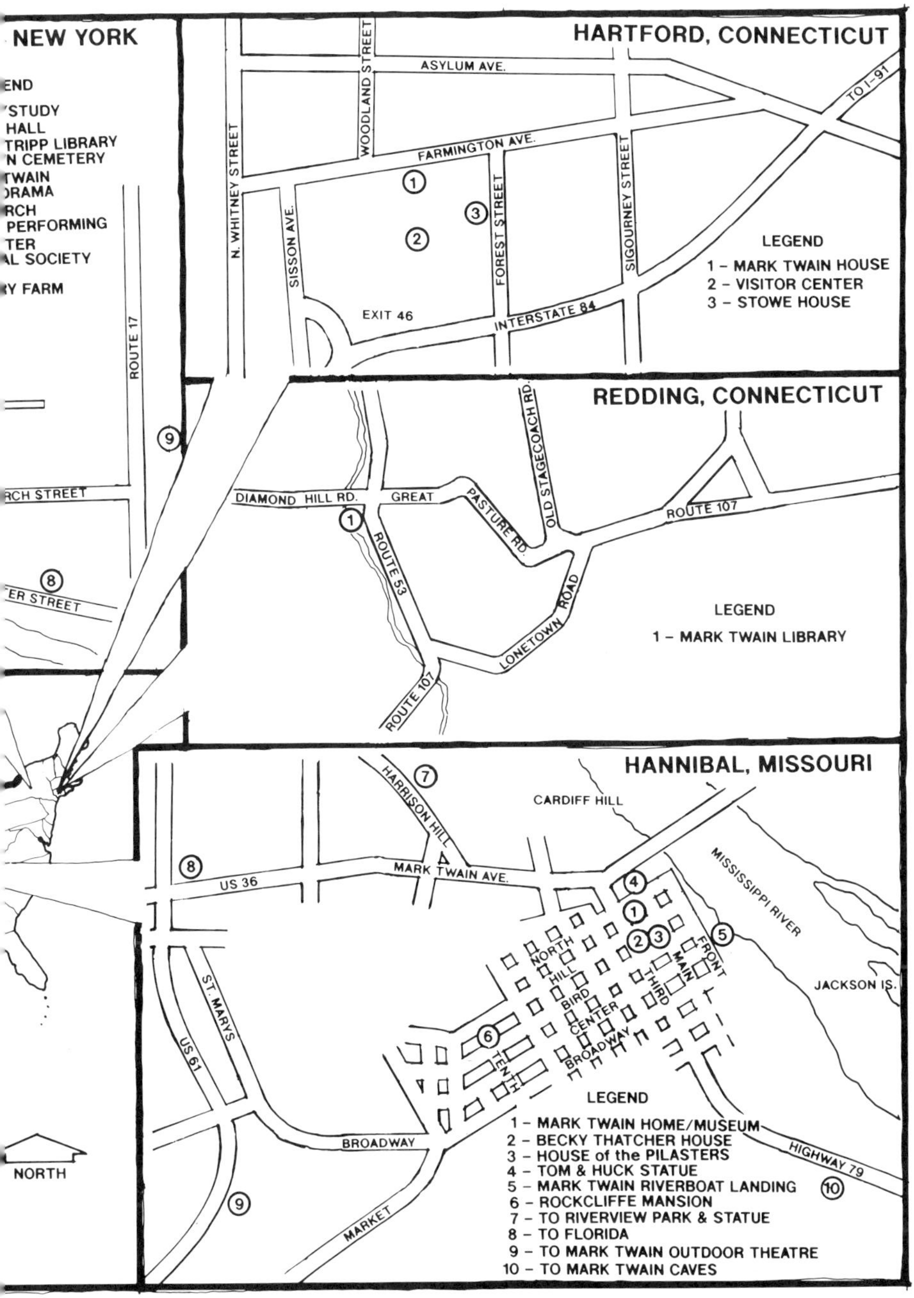

NEW YORK
END
'STUDY
HALL
TRIPP LIBRARY
N CEMETERY
TWAIN
RAMA
RCH
PERFORMING
TER
L SOCIETY
Y FARM
ROUTE 17
RCH STREET
ER STREET
NORTH
HARTFORD, CONNECTICUT
ASYLUM AVE.
WOODLAND STREET
N. WHITNEY STREET
FARMINGTON AVE.
TO I-91
SISSON AVE.
FOREST STREET
SIGOURNEY STREET
EXIT 46
INTERSTATE 84
LEGEND
1 - MARK TWAIN HOUSE
2 - VISITOR CENTER
3 - STOWE HOUSE
REDDING, CONNECTICUT
OLD STAGECOACH RD.
DIAMOND HILL RD.
GREAT
PASTURE RD.
ROUTE 107
ROUTE 53
LONETOWN ROAD
ROUTE 107
LEGEND
1 - MARK TWAIN LIBRARY
HANNIBAL, MISSOURI
HARRISON HILL
CARDIFF HILL
MISSISSIPPI RIVER
US 36
MARK TWAIN AVE.
NORTH
HILL
BIRD
CENTER
BROADWAY
THIRD
MAIN
FRONT
TENTH
JACKSON IS.
ST. MARYS
US 61
BROADWAY
MARKET
HIGHWAY 79
LEGEND
1 - MARK TWAIN HOME/MUSEUM
2 - BECKY THATCHER HOUSE
3 - HOUSE of the PILASTERS
4 - TOM & HUCK STATUE
5 - MARK TWAIN RIVERBOAT LANDING
6 - ROCKCLIFFE MANSION
7 - TO RIVERVIEW PARK & STATUE
8 - TO FLORIDA
9 - TO MARK TWAIN OUTDOOR THEATRE
10 - TO MARK TWAIN CAVES

© 1990

SAN FRANCISCO

In San Francisco Mark Twain found that mix of sophistication and frontier mentality that eventually appreciated his type of humor.

Mark Twain had made several trips to San Francisco as a tourist. To avoid problems with an article he had written in May of 1864 he left Virginia City and headed for San Francisco to live. But, he found it difficult to earn a living there. He had mistakenly thought he would soon make a fortune in stock speculation. By June he had to take a job as a local reporter for the *Daily Morning Call* , but felt overworked. He wrote about every aspect of the city, but was not allowed to write about sensitive subjects. He was unhappy, and sometimes bored, but encouraged by meeting such literary types as Bret Harte. He was "let go" from his position with the *Call* in October. Hundreds of articles were written during that time.

Now, without a regular paycheck, he found himself nearly destitute. He did articles for the *Golden Era* and the *Californian*, literary journals, reviewed plays for the *Dramatic Chronicle* (now the *San Francisco Chronicle*), and wrote for the *Enterprise* in Virginia City. Trouble with the police involving one of his articles prompted him to leave the city for Jackass Hill (see parge 27) in 1864.

And it was in San Francisco, where he launched his career as a lecturer with a speech about Hawaii (see page 31) in 1866.

He even experienced an earthquake. In fact, many of the buildings which stood during Twain's time, including his former office at the *Call*, were destroyed in the great earthquake of 1906.

When Twain was here, over 100 years ago, the Cliff House (sketch on opposite page) was already a tourist attraction. The current building is at the same spectacular site as that visited by Twain, located on the rocky coast where Point Lobos Avenue meets the Great Highway. It was a popular excursion at the time to go at dawn. Twain wrote a wonderfully sarcastic piece about the supposed pleasures of a daybreak trip to watch the sunning seals. He described them as "overgrown maggots". Today the visitor can still enjoy watching cavorting seals from the comfortable bars and restaurants of the Cliff House, call (415) 386-3330.

Across the bay the University of California at Berkeley is home for most of Mark Twain's letters, papers and other documents. The Mark Twain Project, headquartered in The Bancroft Library, is open for scholarly research. Call (415) 642-6480.

THJ
© 1991

JACKASS HILL

Located on Highway 49 between Sonora and Angels Camp is the famed cabin on Jackass Hill where Mark Twain lived and prospected for gold from December, 1864 until February of 1865. Historical markers are placed near the site on highway 49 and a street sign at the road is marked "Jackass Hill Road". About a mile and a half from the turnoff a crude fenced cabin will appear. The most remarkable feature of the cabin is the wonderful stone chimney.

Today the hill seems as if it is the same as when Twain occupied the tiny cabin. The hillside is quite deserted, with but a few roofs of other modest dwellings visible; yet scars on the earth testify to the mining days. This is the same ambiance described by Twain in *Roughing It.* As recently as 1972 a nugget worth close to two thousand dollars was found in the same hole that was once prospected by Mark Twain and the Gillis brothers.

In fact, Twain hated the drudgery of pocket mining and this was a very depressing time for him. He even had thoughts of suicide. It was too cold and rainy to do any digging, so he went to the hotel in Angels Camp (see page 29) and first heard the story of the jumping frog. Back at the cabin he elaborated on the few notes he had taken, and wrote *The Jumping Frog of Calaveras County*, which propelled him to some fame, when it was published in the east.

The Mark Twain cabin located on the hill today is but a replica which was built and dedicated in 1922. A marker at the site was erected by the Tuolumne County Chamber of Commerce in 1929, as part of the Mark Twain Bret Harte Trail. Pictures of the original Gillis cabin indicate there were windows at each side of the door. Despite the crudeness of the surroundings, they had only first-class literature, like Byron and Dickens.

There are no amenities located at the cabin site except for a sole picnic table. Under huge oak trees in the still foothills one can conjure the image of an expectant prospector and writer, Mark Twain.

HOLTON
THJ
© 1991

ANGELS CAMP

Located on Highway 49 only about sixty miles from the Placerville exit off Interstate 80, in the Sierra foothills, is the tiny mining town of Angels Camp. Here, early in 1865, Mark Twain first heard the story of Jim Smiley's frog which he developed into his first widely popular work *The Celebrated Jumping Frog of Calaveras County*. The story appeared in the New York *Saturday Press* in November of 1865. Soon it was being reprinted all over the U.S.A. and Europe and brought him national fame.

When Twain was here it was the cold, rainy and dreary winter of 1865 during the time he lived at Jackass Hill. There was too much rain for mining a nearby claim and he was forced to while away time at the hotel in Angels Camp. He described these adventures in *Roughing It*.

Today the town remains proud of its place in the Mark Twain heritage. Also right off the highway in the center of town is tiny Utica Park graced with lovely trees and a statute of Mark Twain. Highway 49 goes right in front of the building that was site of the Angels Hotel where Twain first heard the frog tale. A stone pedestal in front, on which are mounted a plaque and a bronze frog, helps identify the building. There is also a school, road, and shopping center named after him. Frog items seem popular in the tourist shops.

The most famous event is the annual Jumping Frog Jubilee held in conjunction with the Calaveras County Fair each May. Just a few miles from town is "FROGTOWN" where the fair and contest is held. there is a huge parking lot plus RV parking and camping. The event attracts many motorcycle enthusiasts as well as families. During the Fourth of July a more local event The Mark Twain Days are celebrated as a fund raiser for the hospital, appropriately named the Mark Twain District Hospital in San Andreas. Activities at the fairgrounds include fireworks, a Mark Twain look-alike contest and foodbooths.

In nearby Murphy's, there is a Mark Twain ballroom in the Murphy's hotel named after him, and there is a plaque on the *e. clampus vitus* wall of comparative ovations across the street. The Murphy's Stage Stop Bookstore has an extensive Twain selection.

For more information contact the Calaveras County Chamber of Commerce at (209) 736-4444 or 1-800-999-9039.

THJ
© 1991

HAWAII

In 1866 Mark Twain spent four months in Hawaii. He arrived aboard the steamer *Ajax* on March 18, 1866. He was there as a news reporter,writing travel letters about the Sandwich Islands (as they were called) for the Sacramento *Daily Union.*

His activities were those of today's tourist. He went horseback riding on Oahu, toured Kauai's Waimea Canyon, climbed the crater of Haleakala on Maui, sailed the Kona coast and went hiking around Kilauea volcano. He wrote about vegetation, animals, politics, missionaries and even the economy. He was able to get first word to the mainland about the burning of the ship *Hornet.* That story was widely reprinted and added considerably to his reputation.

Twain left Hawaii on July 19, 1866. When he returned to San Francisco he discovered that he had acquired some fame from his travel letters and the account of the *Hornet* disaster. He was quick to capitalize on his popularity by developing a lecture about the Sandwich Islands which he gave in October, 1866. Thus started Mark Twain's illustrious career as a lecturer. He used the Hawaii material frequently during the next seven years. Today's visitor to Hawaii will still find *Mark Twain's Letters from Hawaii* entertaining and informative.

In the Hawaii Volcano National Park, the Volcano House restaurant and hotel still provide accomodations on the edge of Kilauea. Today's accomodations are more modern and open all year, call (808) 967-7321 for information. A monkeypod tree supposedly planted by Twain at remote Waiohinu was blown down in a storm in 1957, but shoots are said to have reappeared.

On Maui the Haleakala Visitor Center and the Puu Ulaula observation point allow visitors to view the same volcano that once thrilled Mark Twain.

Although the Honolulu area is totally different and developed since Twain's visit, some of the other areas seem little changed from those he described. Several stables offer public horseback riding on Oahu: the Kualoa Ranch, Koko Crater Stables the Turtle Bay Hilton and the New Town and Country Stables.

Twain often claimed that he wanted to get back to Hawaii. He once started a novel set in Hawaii but it was never finished. Mark Twain last saw Hawaii from a ship in the harbor while on a lecture tour in 1895. He could see Honolulu and Diamond Head but a cholera epidemic prevented his landing on the islands he had loved so long.

COOPER UNION
THJ
© 1991

NEW YORK CITY

Samuel Clemens was only seventeen when he arrived in New York City in 1853. He stayed several months, working as a typesetter and exploring the sights. He was attracted to America's first World's Fair and impressed by the Crystal Palace which was located where Bryant Park is today.

Fourteen years later he was back, as Mark Twain, after working as a printer, riverboat pilot, "soldier", secretary, miner, reporter, writer and lecturer. He found the city bigger and more expensive but he stll enjoyed the theatre. He gave a successful lecture about Hawaii in the Great Hall at the Cooper Union in May of 1867. Cooper Union still offers public lectures and exhibits in that same building (sketch on opposite page) at Cooper Square in the East Village. Call (212) 254-6300 for information.

Twain then traveled to Europe and the Holy Land aboard the *Quaker City*. Next he worked in Washington, D.C. (see page 35) and wrote *The Innocents Abroad*, the book which catapulted him to fame.

In New York City, during Christmas 1867, he met Olivia Langdon. He had fallen in love with her picture during his Mediterranean trip. Their first date was to hear Charles Dickens lecture. They married in 1870 and lived in Buffalo, then Hartford and Europe. During those years Twain was a frequent commuter to New York City for business and pleasure. He was a celebrated and prominent figure . His publishing company, Charles L. Webster was on Union Square. His writings were dramatized in the theaters and he was a founding member of The Players, a club at 16 Gramercy Park, where he often stayed. His gala seventieth birthday party was celebrated at Delmonico's Restaurant, which is now gone.

A plaque at 14 West 10th Street marks the building where he lived in 1900. There is another marker at 21 Fifth Avenue, site of the building where he lived from 1904 until 1908.

In 1910 Mark Twain's funeral at the Brick Presbyterian Church, which was then on Fifth Avenue, was so crowded that the street was blocked by people!

A Mark Twain Birthday Tour on the last weekend in November is conducted by author and Mark Twain expert, Peter Salwen for $10.00. The walking tour features sights and readings from Mark Twain's New York and is also available by special arrangement, call (212) 242-5546.

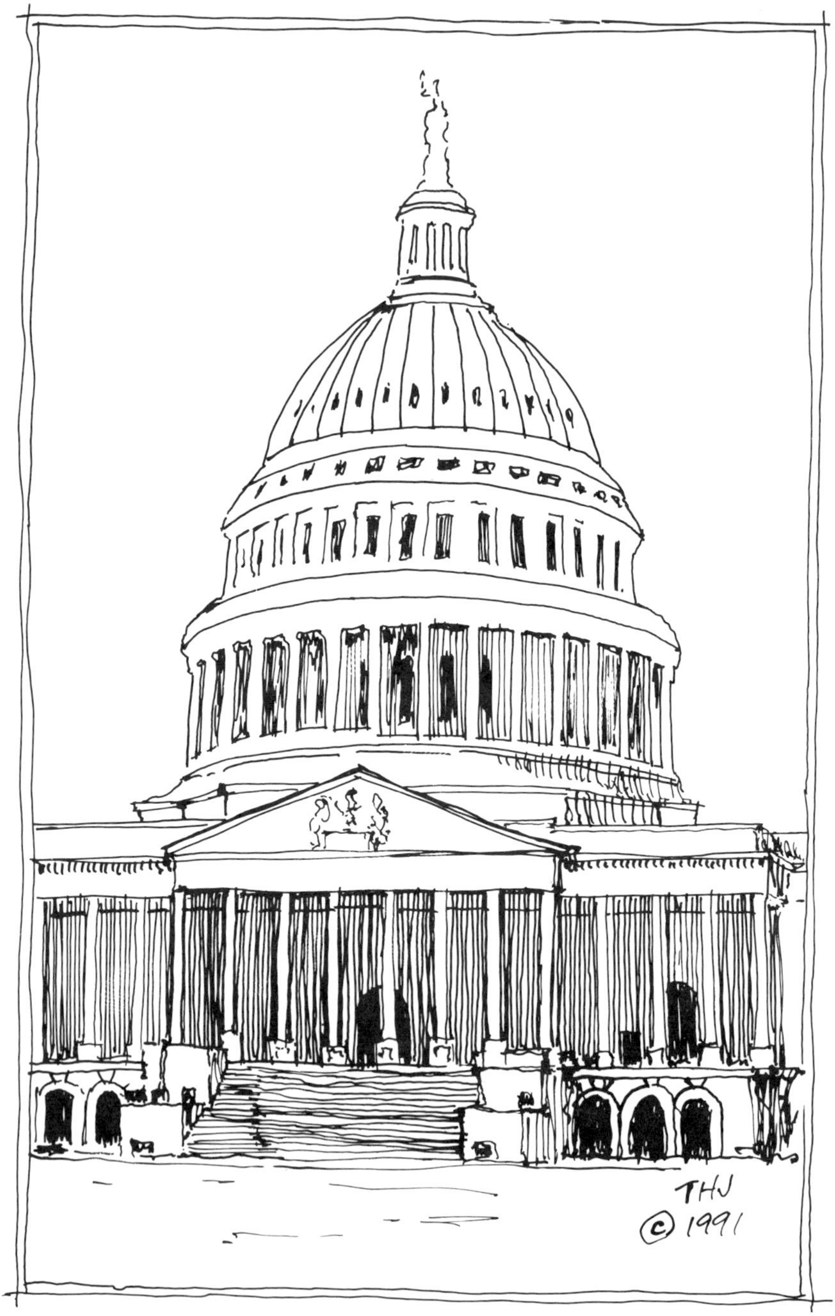
THJ
© 1991

WASHINGTON, D.C.

There is definitly a political essence to many of the writings of Mark Twain so it's only logical that his connections to Washington, D. C. spanned his youth to old age.

Young Samuel Clemens was only 18 years old when he first visited the nations' Capitol as a tourist for a few days in February 1854. He was working as a printer in Philadelphia and was also writng travel letters to Orion's paper in Iowa, the Muscatine *Journal.* He was a great sightseer and reported on the Capitol Building (sketch on opposite page), the Smithsonian Institute, the Washington Monument and his special favorite, The Museum of the Patent Office.. Samuel L. Clemens was also an inventor and was issued three patents during his life. One was for a scrapbook with self-adhesive pages, and another for a memory-builder game. Today the Old Patent Office building houses the National Portrait Gallery on 8th Street at F Street, NW.

After his experiences as a riverboat pilot, private secretary to The Secretary of the Nevada Territory (his brother Orion), newsreporter, editor and travel correspondent it was not so odd that in 1867 Mark Twain landed the postion of private secretary to Senator William M. Stewart of Nevada. Twain was also writing *The Innocents Abroad*, the book that established his career. There was a falling out with the Senator but Twain then worked for several newspapers and lived in various boardinghouses in Washington. One of these was the Ebbett House.

In 1873 he wrote a novel with Charles Dudley Warner called *The Gilded Age* in which he described the almost surrealistic experiences induced by the political atmosphere in the Capitol.

Twain and his friend from the California days, Bret Harte collaborated on the play *Ah Sin* which opened (somewhat unsuccessfully) at the National Theatre in 1877. Today the National Theatre has been restored and continues to operate. Call 1-800-233-3123 for tickets.

Mark Twain's most dramatic appearance in Washington was to testify before the House Committee on Copyrights in 1906. Wearing his white suit, he testified in favor of more protection for authors. He thought that protection should extend for fifty years beyond the author's death. He would probably be satisfied to know that that is the law today.

THJ
© 1990

ELMIRA

It was love that first brought Mark Twain to Elmira, New York, in 1868. He had met Charles Langdon during his Holy Land trip. Twain claimed to have fallen in love with Charles' sister, Olivia, when he first saw her picture. He seemed rough, unpolished and worldly for the delicate, cultured and wealthy, young lady. Her family, however, grew to like him and he eventually prevailed. Samuel Clemens (as he is commonly referred to in Elmira) and Olivia Langdon were married at her home in Elmira on February 2, 1870.

The Langdon family had a luxurious Victorian mansion on North Main Street. The house was demolished in 1939 to make room for the Langdon Plaza shopping center. (Destruction was controversial, but there was not enough money for renovations.)

In addition to the formal city home, the family owned Quarry Farm, on East Hill about two miles from the bustling, industrial city. The tranquil farm with its misty Chemung River valley view was where the Clemens family stayed during their summers in Elmira. Daughter Clara was born at the farm in 1874. Children, cats, vegetation and writing all thrived in that bucolic setting.

A small octogon shaped building (sketch on opposite page) was built in 1874. It was for Twain to use as a private study at Quarry Farm. The tiny window-lined study commanded a grand view of the lush rolling hills. In that isolated place Mark Twain did some of his best writing. There he created such characters as Huck Finn and Tom Sawyer and wrote *The Prince and the Pauper* and *A Connecticut Yankee in King Arthur's Court.* The study was moved to the Elmira College campus in 1952. Quarry Farm is now a Mark Twain Research Center, not open to the public.

In town, Mark Twain enjoyed drinks, billiards and cigars with friends at Klapproth's Tavern which is partially reconstructed in the Gannett-Tripp Library on the Elmira College campus. The progressive Reverend Thomas Beecher of the Park Congregational Church, was a life-long friend. Although Twain lectured several times in Elmira he was never asked to speak at Elmira College.

Samuel L. Clemens and his family are buried in the Langdon family plot in Woodlawn Cemetery.

See page 43 for details about other Twain attractions. For more information about Elmira call the Chemung County Chamber of Commerce at 1-(800)-MARK TWAIN.

© 1990

HARTFORD

The Mark Twain House and Memorial in Hartford, Connecticut is located at 351 Farmington Avenue. It is built of ornate brick in an intellectual retreat called Nook Farm, which also includes the Harriet Beecher Stowe House.

Mark Twain was impressed when he visited Hartford on business in 1868. Hartford was home to the American Publishing Company which published *The Innocents Abroad* in 1869 and *Roughing It* in 1872.

It was the refined literary and cultural milieu that attracted the young family to Hartford, after a devastating year and a half in Buffalo (see page 9). Mark Twain spent two decades, from 1871 to 1891 in Hartford and those were among the happiest years in his life.

The nineteen room home, designed by architect E. T. Potter, was completed in 1874. Although a study had been built for Twain to write in, he found that he could not work there! Eventually he moved a writing table to the top floor billiard room. In that room he wrote about Tom Sawyer and Huckleberry Finn. During this period he also published *The Prince and the Pauper*, *Life on the Mississippi*, and *A Connecticut Yankee in King Arthur's Court*.

His wife Livy, three daughters and servants provided a complete picture of elegant domestic bliss. They loved their home and felt it had a heart and soul of its own. It was beautifully decorated, with stained glass by Tiffany. For nearly twenty years Livy's investments and Twain's writings and business ventures, including publishing, succeded in supporting the family. Unfortunately, the house, their lifestyle and entertainments were expensive to maintain.

Twain was also an inventor and interested in new gadgets. He held several patents. But Twain made a poor investment in the Paige typesetting machine. In 1891 business reverses caused the family to leave for Europe where they could live more economically. Daughter Susy died in the house in 1896 and it was sold in 1903.

The house was purchased by the Mark Twain Memorial and Library Commission in 1929 and has been completely restored. The site includes the Stowe House and a museum shop. Open all year, admission is $6.50 for adults and $2.75 for children and includes an hour-long guided tour. An exhibit hall contains memorabilia, including the infamous Paige typesetting machine. For additional information call (203) 525-9317.

THJ
© 1991

REDDING

Redding, Connecticut is located in the wooded hill country of southwestern Connecticut. It was this tranquil setting that Mark Twain chose for his last home. In 1906 he purchased 200 acres and built the house which he called "Stormfield" after his work *Captain Stormfield's Visit to Heaven.* The success of that work helped him pay for the estate.

His final home had a billiard room decorated in red, numerous guest rooms and a large living room which contained a mechanical orchestrelle. He moved into the house on June 18, 1908. The local citizenry held a "parade" on that day, escorting him to his new home from the train station in flower decorated carriages! The next year and a half were to be happy for Mark Twain; who was still grieving from the loss of his beloved wife, Livy. He played billiards and worked on his memoirs with his biographer, Albert Bigelow Paine. His daughter Clara was married to the famous musician, Ossip Gabrilowitsch at "Stormfield" and they were expecting his first grandchild (she was born after he died). Mark Twain was instrumental in establishing the town library which still bears his name. He hosted a fund raising concert at "Stormfield" and donated volumes from his personal collections as well as cash proceeds from his daughter Jeans' estate.

It was the tragic death of Jean Clemens, of an epileptic fit while bathing on Christmas eve 1909, that lead to the final decline of Mark Twain himself. He was too ill to accompany her body to Elmira, New York for burial. A few months later, on April 21, 1910, Samuel Clemens died at "Stormfield". Overhead, Halley's comet steaked through the sky. His funeral was held in New York City and he was laid to rest in Elmira, New York (see page 43).

On July 25, 1923 "Stormfield" was destroyed by fire. A similar house was built on the same foundations. It is privately owned and not open to the public.

Today the little town of Redding is still proud of its Mark Twain Library which opened in February, 1911. A public library seems to be an especially appropriate memorial for so popular a writer. The library is located on Route 53 in Redding and was renovated in 1990. It contains volumes from Twain's own library, and a few pieces of Twain memorabilia. For more information, call (203) 938-2545.

LANGDON
THJ
© 1991

ELMIRA

Mark Twain was buried in Woodlawn Cemetery in Elmira, New York in 1910. He is in the Langdon family plot (sketch on opposite page) with his wife, four children, son-in-law and grandchild. A small, simple marker identifies his grave with both names: Clemens and Twain. The cemetery is open from 8:00am until 9:00pm and visitors are welcome.

The Mark Twain legacy is evident almost everywhere in Elmira (also see page 37). The most significant single building is his study, now conveniently located on the Elmira College campus on Park Place, at College and Washington Avenues. The tiny octogon-shaped building is open to visitors in the summer, and can easily be peered into when closed. Across the street, in Hamilton Hall, a Mark Twain exhibit and slide show describes Twain's days in Elmira. There is even a partial reconstruction of his favorite tavern, Klapproth's, in the Gannett-Tripp Library on the campus.

Today Quarry Farm, on Crane Road, is site of The Center for Mark Twain Studies. It is not open to the public, in order to maintain the same undisturbed setting for its resident scholars that Mark Twain once enjoyed. It sponsors school programs, scholarly research and public lectures, call (607) 732-0993 for schedules.

Park Congregational Church, where Twain's friend Thomas Beecher preached, is across from Langdon Plaza on Church Street.

McGraw Bookstore on campus and Bookmarks, downtown in Clemens Square, both carry books by and about Mark Twain.

The Trolley into Mark Twain Country runs during the summer months. It offers an excellent ninty-minute tour of Elmira and is a bargain at $2.00 for adults with children under twelve free. Call (607) 734-5137 for information.

From early July until Labor Day weekend, a Mark Twain Musical Drama is presented in a 1500 seat air-conditioned geodesic dome. The Domes theatre is several miles north of Elmira (on Route 14) in the Mark Twain State Park. The set features a life-size replica of the house at Quarry Farm. For reservations call 1-(800) 336-MARK or (607) 796-4111.

The Chemung County Historical Society has some Twain exhibits, call (607) 734-4167. There is also a Mark Twain Riverfront Park, Clemens Performing Arts Center, Clemens Square and Clemens Center Parkway. For more information call 1 (800)- MARK TWAIN.

BIBLIOGRAPHY

Branch, Edgar M., ed., *Clemens of the Call: Mark Twain in San Francisco*, Berkeley and Los Angeles, University of California Press, 1969.

Day, A. Grove, ed., *Mark Twain's Letters From Hawaii*, Honolulu, The University Press of Hawaii, 1975.

DeVoto, Bernard, *Mark Twain's America*, Moscow, University of Idaho Press, 1932.

Fatout, Paul, *Mark Twain on the Lecture Circuit*, Carbondale and Edwardsville, Southern Illinois University Press, 1969.

Jerome, Robert D. and Herbert A. Wisbey, Jr., *Mark Twain in Elmira*, Elmira, Mark Twain Society, Inc., 1977.

Kaplan, Justin, *Mark Twain and His World*, New York, Simon and Schuster, 1974.

Kaplan, Justin, *Mr. Clemens and Mark Twain*, New York, Simon and Schuster, 1966.

Lauber, John, *The Inventions of Mark Twain: A Biography*, New York, Hill and Wang, 1990.

Lennon, Nigey, *Mark Twain in California*, San Francisco, Chronicle Books, 1982.

Meltzer, Milton, *Mark Twain Himself*, New York, Bonanza Books, 1960.

Neider, Charles, ed., *The Selected Letters of Mark Twain*, New York, Harper & Row, Publishers, 1982.

Paine, Albert Bigelow, *Mark Twain: A Biography*, New York, Harper and Brothers Publishers, 1912.

Salwen, Peter, "Mark Twain, The New Yorker", New York, *New York Newsday*, November 29, 1985.

Sanborn, Margaret, *Mark Twain: The Bachelor Years*, New York, Doubleday, 1990.

Twain, Mark, *Mark Twain's Autobiography*, New York, P.F. Collier and Son Company, 1924.

Wecter, Dixon, *Sam Clemens of Hannibal*, Cambridge, The Riverside Press, 1952.

Williams, George III, *Mark Twain: His Life in Virginia City, Nevada*, Riverside, California, Tree By The River Publishing, 1985.

Williams, George III, *Mark Twain: Jackass Hill and the Jumping Frog*, Dayton, Nevada, Tree By The River Publishing, 1988.